THIS JOURNAL IS
THE FUCKING PROPERTY OF:

_____

Published by Sourcebooks
P.O. Box 4410, Naperville, Illinois 60567-4410
(630) 961-3900
sourcebooks.com

Printed and bound in the United States of America.

VP 10 9 8 7 6 5 4 3 2

A F*cking Rage Journal

Warning:
Destruction
Ahead

A Fucking Rage Journal

When life gives you lemons—and there sure seems to be an endless supply of fucking lemons—forget making lemonade and instead embark on a journey of mass destruction...of a journal.

We introduce you to *A Fucking Rage Journal*. Use this journal to unleash your rage, frustrations, pent-up aggressions, irritations, bothers, annoyances, and any other shit that needs to be let out. Get your negative thoughts and feelings on the page and **RAGE** with abandon.

This journal is for the people who are always internally screaming. For the people who always keep negative shit bottled up inside. For the people who wish they had a healthy outlet. And, of course, for the people who just really like raging and fucking shit up.

Proceed without caution.

Hierarchy of Destruction

Fucking the journal up unrecognizably & beyond repair

Obliterating the pages because now shit's personal

Declaring the journal your mortal enemy

Doing more shit than the activities suggest

Fucking up some pages

Answering some questions

Reading the journal

Ways to Fuck This Journal Up

This is in no way a comprehensive list of ways to fuck this journal up. Be creative. Add shit wherever you see fit.

- Burn (safely, of course)
- Tear (always delightful)
- Rip out pages (so many options)
- Deface the pages (oddly cathartic)
- Scribble (highly encouraged)
- Throw it around (at the walls, floors, ground, people—who can say?)
- Leave it outside for a while (nature has a wicked sense of humor)
- Stick it in random locations (fridges, attics, basements, the ground)
- Dunk it in water (eh, sure it'll dry)
- Infuse it with smells (good or bad, it's really up to you)
- Use it to collect shit (receipts, used gum, candy wrappers, fingernails)

Goeth & Fucketh
This Journal Up

Before you embark on your journey of destruction and inspiration, it's important to remind yourself of a few things:

—— I give myself permission to unleash my rage.

—— I embrace the opportunity to release my thoughts and feelings in this safe space.

—— I acknowledge that this journal is a tool for expressing negative feelings in unharmful ways.

—— I accept that there is no wrong way to approach this journal.

—— I vow that not a single page will be left intact.

If you can't promise anything else, just promise this:

—— I solemnly swear that this journal will be fucked up at the end of this.

Now, begin the journal any way you damn please.

If **ANGER** were a color,
what would it be?

Drown the whole damn page in the color.

Make a list of shit that **PISSES** you off.
(You'll probably have to narrow this down
to whatever you can fit on the page.)

If you could convince
literally everyone of just one
fucking thing, what would it be?

Who are some people who just really fucking irritate you?

Bonus points if you explain why!

Sorry,
I checked
my receipt
& I actually
didn't buy
any of your
bullshit.

Minor Inconvenience Rating Scale

On a scale of 1 to 10, rate how much these everyday inconveniences bother the shit out of you. (Or just create your own damn scale. Fuck the rules.)

___ When you hit every single fucking red light when coming home after a very long day.

___ When you just miss charging your phone in time.

___ When you're just about to go to sleep, and then you remember that **ONE** thing you forgot to do.

___ When you sit down to relax and can't find your headphones.

___ When the Wi-Fi randomly stops working. (Why the fuck do you pay for this shit?)

___ When you realize the floor is wet for some ridiculous reason, and you're wearing socks.

___ When you **KNOW YOUR PASSWORD,** and it still **SAYS YOU'RE WRONG.**

___ When someone eats the last of your favorite snack.

___ When you wake up before your alarm and realize you've lost out on precious moments of sleep.

___ When people park like assholes, and you can't find a parking spot.

___ When you run out of shampoo or conditioner but somehow never both at the same time. (Shit's a conspiracy.)

___ When you forget to replace the toilet paper roll, and you've already sat down. (Well, shit.)

___ When, despite your best efforts, you can never fucking find your wallet when you need it.

___ When they decide to rearrange the whole grocery store for literally no reason. (Who do those assholes think they are?)

___ When you're washing the dishes, and you accidentally touch a piece of food (and you die a little inside).

___ When you're trying to sleep, but someone is snoring loudly nearby.

___ When you're trying to go somewhere, and the person in front of you is **SO SLOW** for no damn reason.

___ When you had plans you were excited about, and someone cancels last minute.

___ When the neighbors are loud as hell on a weekday night with no damn consideration for others. (See: fucking fireworks at 2:00 a.m.)

___ When people consider themselves above using turn signals.

___ When you've unsubscribed 1,000 times already, and you **STILL** get emails.

___ When you hold the door open for someone and they don't say "thank you."

___ When people stand in the aisles as soon as the plane lands as if they can leave immediately. (Like, where the fuck do you think you're going to go?)

___ When you're trying to enjoy the movie, and people are talking or playing on their phones. (Movies are too expensive for this type of shit.)

___ When people try to cut you in line.

___ When you're watching TV or videos on your phone, and the sound suddenly gets out of sync and you just have to give up.

If **ANGER** had a taste, what would it be?

ck Up This Page!

Shove a sample of the taste on the page.

Take a bite if you really want to...we don't care.

What's one quote that really sums
up your frustrations right now?
You can make it up if you want.

Is there anything you can do to get rid of those frustrations?

If not, go ahead and take it out on this page.

What are the top three things you
absolutely fucking detest about Mondays?

1

2

3

Being friendly is vastly fucking overrated.

☐ Agree

☐ Disagree

Write an essay about why it should be illegal for people to talk to you before you've had coffee or woken up properly.

Unfortunately, the struggle is, as they say, fucking **REAL.**
What are some of the hardest things you've ever done?

You're a
fucking badass
for getting
through them

If **ANGER** was a smell,
what would it be?

Infuse this page with perfume, hairspray,
essential oils, or fucking spaghetti sauce—
whatever you feel best represents anger.

Let's set the fucking record straight

I AM NOT

↓

I AM

What would you do if you won the lottery? (Before you book a one-way flight and run the hell away from everything, of course.)

Write down things you need to let go of. Cut out everything and rip, shred, and burn to your heart's content.

Let go of the heavy shit—

you'll hurt your damn back carrying all that weight.

Use this page as a tissue the next time you cry.
Drown it in tears and snot.

One day,
you'll make
the fucking
onions cry
instead.
That'll show 'em.

Fuck-It List

You've heard of bucket lists. We now introduce you to the new and improved Fuck-It List. Write down anything you just can't stand about your life right now, so you can stop that shit and make your life enjoyable again, damn it!

(Don't) Think Fast!

No, this activity will not reveal any secrets of your unconscious or uncover any mysterious messages nestled deep in your psyche.

We're not Sigmund fucking Freud (thankfully).

Just jot down whatever word first comes to mind when you read each of these words. (We'll know if you're cheating. Don't question it.)

LOVE /

FEAR /

ANGER /

SAD /

HAPPY /

LIFE /

DEATH /

EVERYTHING /

NOTHING /

TECHNOLOGY /

MUSIC /

MEDICINE /

WATER /

DANCE /

MISTAKE /

FOOD /

BOLD /

BEAUTIFUL /

SORRY /

FAITH /

FAMILY /

FRIENDS /

COOL /

HATE /

AVOID /

ORIGINAL /

LIGHT /

DARK /

SHADOW /

MIND /

SHARE /

PASSION /

HELPLESS /

PURPOSE /

CHANGE /

DARE /

HUNGRY /

AMBITION /

After completing the word association activity,
did any response stand out to you? Cross out anything
that doesn't fucking resonate, and circle what does.

Fortune
favors
the badass!

Write down some moments
that were **RUINED** for you.

Now it's time to **RUIN** this page with everything you fucking have. Go wild.

What is your most controversial opinion?

What feelings does this opinion evoke?

Why is it controversial?

DON'T HOLD BACK!

What are some things you have to do that
you think are just the biggest **WASTES OF TIME**?

What are some **TALENTS** you have?

And don't you dare write "nothing."

You must have some outlet for all that badassery.

What's some of the most embarrassing shit
you've ever been a fan of? Write it down.
WRITE IT ALL DOWN.

What's some shit that really just grinds your gears? Any pet peeves?

When was the last time you got the **LAST LAUGH**?
Remind yourself of how that felt.

What does **ANGER** feel like?

ck Up This Page!

Pretend this page did something terrible to wrong you.
It's time to take sweet, sweet revenge on this page.

(Fuck you, page.)

When did you realize that you'd grown up (or that you hadn't)? Tap into any feelings of rage, bitterness, or disappointment and **LET IT ALL OUT** on the page.

Turn this page into a toy. Make a paper airplane. Fold it into an origami crane. Cut it up into one of those paper snowflakes. Whatever floats your fucking boat.

Remember when you used to draw these?

You're the real fucking MVP

This is a page for all your fucking favorite **SWEAR WORDS** and phrases. How creative can you be?

Write about a friend who turned out to be a liar, backstabber, or otherwise just-not-great fucking person.

Take this page and slam-dunk it in the trash.

Rated A for Abso-fucking-lutely Awesome

What star rating would you give yourself for each of the attributes listed below?

☆☆☆☆☆☆ KINDNESS

☆☆☆☆☆☆ INTELLIGENCE

☆☆☆☆☆☆ DILIGENCE

☆☆☆☆☆☆ LOYALTY

☆☆☆☆☆☆ ATTRACTIVENESS

☆☆☆☆☆☆ GENUINENESS

☆☆☆☆☆☆ GOOFINESS

☆☆☆☆☆☆ CREATIVITY

☆☆☆☆☆☆ ACCEPTANCE

☆☆☆☆☆☆ STRENGTH

☆☆☆☆☆☆ FRIENDLINESS

☆☆☆☆☆☆ FLEXIBILITY

☆☆☆☆☆☆ NURTURING

☆☆☆☆☆☆ THOUGHTFULNESS

☆☆☆☆☆☆ CONFIDENCE

☆☆☆☆☆☆ OPTIMISM

☆☆☆☆☆☆ RESPECTFULNESS

☆☆☆☆☆☆ DETERMINEDNESS

☆☆☆☆☆☆ HELPFULNESS

☆☆☆☆☆☆ MOTIVATION

☆☆☆☆☆☆ INSIGHT

☆☆☆☆☆☆ HUMOR

☆☆☆☆☆☆ PATIENCE

☆☆☆☆☆ HONESTY

☆☆☆☆☆ GENEROSITY

☆☆☆☆☆ MODESTY

☆☆☆☆☆ SERIOUSNESS

☆☆☆☆☆ INDEPENDENCE

☆☆☆☆☆ TRUST

☆☆☆☆☆ RESILIENCE

☆☆☆☆☆ RELIABILITY

☆☆☆☆☆ RELAXEDNESS

☆☆☆☆☆ LISTENING

☆☆☆☆☆ COURAGE

☆☆☆☆☆ DECISIVENESS

☆☆☆☆☆ ENTHUSIASM

☆☆☆☆☆ FORGIVENESS

☆☆☆☆☆ SENSITIVITY

☆☆☆☆☆ ORGANIZATION

☆☆☆☆☆ PRACTICALITY

☆☆☆☆☆ MATURITY

☆☆☆☆☆ FOCUS

☆☆☆☆☆ COURTESY

☆☆☆☆☆ OPEN-MINDEDNESS

☆☆☆☆☆ POSITIVITY

☆☆☆☆☆ RESPONSIBILITY

Hope you were fucking honest with yourself, unlike some online reviewers. Are there any attributes here you'd like to develop or improve?

Write down some things that **ANNOY YOU** about
your personality. Cross all that shit out in red.
You don't need that kind of negativity in your life.

Cover this fucking page fucking completely
with the fucking word **FUCK.**

Write down some shit that **SCARES** you.

Draw all over this spread with black ink, crayon, or paint.

Blot out all your fears. They're not in fucking charge here.

With this journal as your only witness, brain-dump about some shit that's been upsetting you recently.

Rip this page out and bury it somewhere
no one will ever find it.

Looks like it's cloudy with a chance of bullshit.

What are some things you think about before you go to sleep? Don't be shy. Be weird as hell here if you want.

If you're having trouble sleeping, throw in a brainstorm of calmer or nicer things you can think about or do before bed.

Things that fill me with rage

What are some things that never fail to make you **RAGE**? Are there healthier ways to deal with that anger? Any other coping strategies you can think of?

ck Up This Page!

Write down a few things you're raging about right now
on this page. Stomp on the page for good measure
before you tear that shit out of the journal.

Have you ever wanted to throw your drink in some asshole's face like they always do in the movies?

Here's your fucking chance.

Toss your soda, coffee, milkshake, or whatever's your cup of tea here. Imagine it splashing into the face of someone who deserves it.

Be a
constant
fucking
delight.

What do you always end up procrastinating on?
Are you procrastinating right now? (Don't lie!)

What are some things that keep
you motivated to stay on track?

Let's engage with and heal your inner child. (That cute-ass kiddo deserves some love, damn it!) What were some of your favorite activities to do when you were younger? Do you still enjoy doing any of them?

Now it's time for the time-honored tradition of
FINGER PAINTING. Dip your fingers, hands,
or feet (if you must) in paint, peanut butter,
egg yolk, mud, whatever the fuck is on hand,
and create your true masterpiece.

You beautiful bastard.

Who are your anti-role models?
People you **NEVER** want to be like?

Who are your role models? (This can be you.)

What makes you feel **ALIVE**? Make a plan below to incorporate more of that shit into your life pronto.

Transform this page into something you can use as part
of a game. Make it a ball to catch or kick. Use it
as a chessboard. Create your own damn game and rules.

Well, that's life.

(Fuck!)

What are some habits you've picked up that
you wish you could **FUCKING STOP?**

Eclectic Collector

What are some of your passionate interests? Nerdy interests? Things you just can't help but obsess over?

How do these interests provide an outlet for your feelings?

Fill this entire page with imagery or items representing your favorite interests or hobbies. Completely overwhelm the page. Make it unusable. It's just you and your interests.

Do you feel like anything is missing in your life?
Write about any holes in your life, and brainstorm
some healthy ways to fill them.

Holy shit, this page is holey!

Puncture this page with holes.

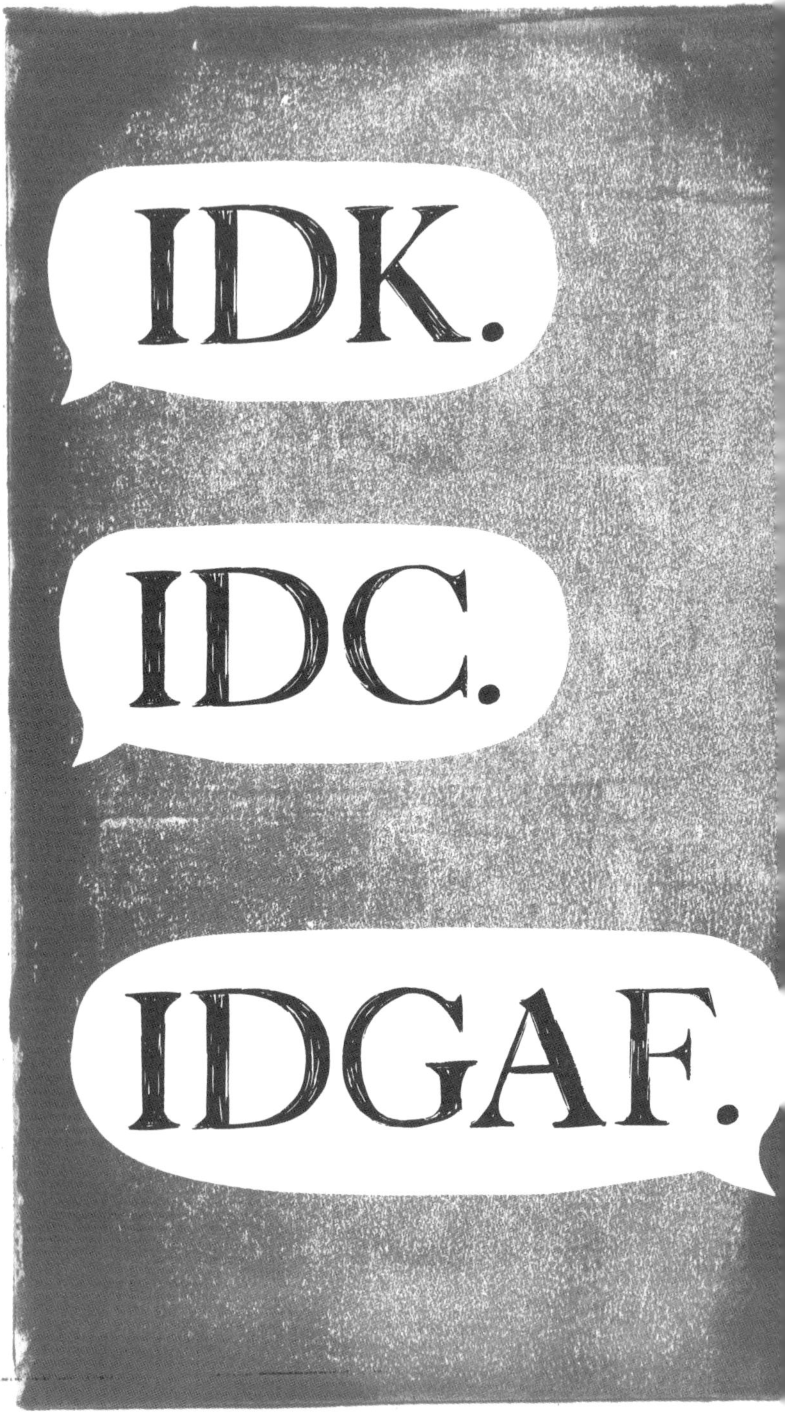
IDK.
IDC.
IDGAF.

What are some things you still feel guilty for?

How do you handle any guilt you may carry?

Is it time to let any of that go?

What's some advice you wish you'd never taken?

What is some advice you wish you had gotten before you first experienced something, whether that be a new school, career opportunity, move, or other point of change in your life.

Scribble out your pent-up frustrations.

Loop-de-loop the fuck out of this page.

Here's an incomplete list of actions and experiences designed to get you to let your aggression out!

What else can you think of to add to the list?

☐ Go to a rage room and **LET FUCKING LOOSE**.

☐ Walk or drive over to a field or otherwise empty area and scream your fucking heart out.

☐ Smash something against the wall—
watch out for any broken shit.

☐ Get into a heated argument with yourself so you can verbalize everything you need to say!

☐ Sing fucking **AGGRESSIVELY**.

☐

☐

☐

☐

☐

☐

☐

What are some of your favorite
things to **COMPLAIN** about?

Fuckety fuck f
ck fuck fuck fu
uck fuck fuck f
k fuck fuck fu
uck fuck fuck
ck fuck fuck fu
fuck fuck fuc
uck fuck fuck f
k fuck fuck fu
uck fuck fuck.

Write about some things that are **EATING YOU UP** inside.
What can you do about them?

Use this page to document your favorite foods.

What you had for breakfast or dinner. Your favorite snack.

Make this page as tasty as you damn well please.

Life is
10%
what happens
to you and
90%
how many
times you
say "shit"
throughout it.

When was the last time you felt in control?

Replicate that shit

When was the last time you failed at something? How did that make you feel? When did you realize that it doesn't matter in the long run because **YOU'RE A TOTAL BADASS**?

Channel your inner obnoxious teacher and ruthlessly grade this blank page. Write *F*s in thick red ink. Make up criticisms for an invisible essay. **IT'S FUCKING PAYBACK TIME.**

What are some things in your life that you **REGRET**?
How do you cope with that regret?

Tear this page out and roast it in a fire like you would a marshmallow. Be mindful of the damn flames.

Transcend the *bullshit.*

What are some things that work
as distractions from your anger?

What always works to mellow you out
after a long and frustrating day?

What is a letter you'll never send? Why?

Now, write that damn letter. Then burn it, drown it,
cross it out. Do whatever feels right to you.

MY LAST FUCK!

Oh look, it's on fire.

Do you enforce boundaries, or do
you tend to let people cross the line?
How does that make you feel?

Do you ever feel misunderstood?
What misconceptions do people
seem to have about you?

Throw this page or the whole damn journal
from the highest point you can safely reach.

Hold on,
let me
fucking
overthink
everything.

What **EMOTIONS** do you have the most difficulty grappling with? Where does that come from?

COLOR IN
OR RIP
THE SHIT
OUT OF THE EDGES.

DEFACE
THE
TITLE
PAGE.

*Destroy
the
cover.*

Go fucking ham
on any page that
pisses you off.

STEP 1: Coat this page with glue.
   STEP 2: COVER it in glitter.
OPTIONAL: Leave page in journal.

Warning:
Glitter may
never
go away

Salty.
As.
Fuck.

Who or what has the most influence on you?
Is this healthy?

Who do you **ENVY**? Why?

What can you do to feel more contentment?

Make a green smoothie with this page!
Tear it out and make like a blender!
Dye this page green with food coloring
or a green liquid of your choice. Shred it up.
(We don't advise consuming it.)

The grind *never* fucking stops.

What is something you've vowed to never do again?
Will you really hold yourself to it?

Rage Painting

Make a splatter painting across this spread.

1

Prop this journal up.

2

Wet a brush with some paint.

3

Stand back.

4

Splatter the paint on the journal.
Splatter it like you really
fucking mean it.

Shit could be worse?

What is one thing you'd do **ANYTHING** to have
if life would just stop fucking getting in the way?

Fly off
the Candle

Take this opportunity to combine your
passion for candles and fucking
your journal up beyond repair!
(Mind the damn wax!)

Drop
candle wa
on this
spread

Have you ever stepped on someone else
to get ahead, or has someone done this to you?
How did it make you feel?

ck Up This Page!

Stand on this page. Muddy shoes are preferable.
Stomp on it a few times until the pages get crushed.

Has anyone's actions ever created hate or deep rage within you? Like, not mild anger but a deep and seemingly unrelenting anger. Are you still holding on to that feeling? Why?

Visualize your hateful feelings as this journal.

Tie a string to this journal or fucking attach a rope to it.

Swing it around to your heart's content.

If you could **SWAP LIVES** with someone else, who would you choose and why?

Rip out this page. Disfigure it beyond recognition.

Reattach it somewhere else in the journal.

Blow off some damn steam.

Well, isn't this a clusterfuck?

Name something that you **SECRETLY JUDGE** about others. Why do you focus on that?

Take this journal to the park, the beach, the lake,
the forest preserve—wherever the hell it can get dirty.
Let Mother Nature do whatever the fuck she wants to it.

Have you ever been physically or emotionally aggressive
with someone? Why? How did you feel afterward?
Was there a healthier approach to the situation?

_____

_____

_____

_____

_____

_____

_____

_____

_____

_____

_____

_____

_____

_____

_____

_____

_____

_____

When it comes down to it, who will really be there for you? Write about a time when you needed someone and they weren't there for you.

Fuck this
page up
as needed

SIIIIIIIII
IIIIIIIIIIIIIII
IIIIIIIIIIIIII
IIIIIIIIIGG
GGGGGG
GGGHHH
HHHHHHHH
HHHHHHH
HHHHHHH

What are some memories from your past that still affect
you today? How do these memories shape your beliefs,
behaviors, and relationships?

Is it okay for you to be lazy? Why or why not?

Does the laziness of others piss you off?

Use this page or the whole fucking journal
to complete a chore, like sweeping the floors
or washing the walls.

What kinds of situations make you withdraw
or feel fucking depressed? How does your body react?

Submerge this page in a liquid of your choice. Leave it out
in the sun to dry. Stick it back into the journal.

Oh, look.
It's
I-don't-
give-a-shit
o'clock.

When was the last time you fought with family members?

What was it about and what triggered it?

How did it make you feel?

What is something that you've heard recently that
has stuck with you? Why? What is the significance?

Stick sticky things here.

Yes, even if they're fucking gross.

...and there was not a single fuck given that day.

Are you ever rude on purpose?
Why does that happen?

Use this page as a safe space to complain about your parents, guardians, boss, or whatever authority figure you have in your life. (We won't tell if you won't tell.)

What are your most toxic traits? How can you work to transform your toxic traits into healthier traits that allow you to unleash your badass self?

Are you able to forgive yourself for mistakes?
Why or why not? Do you forgive others more easily
than you forgive yourself?

When did you feel most betrayed and why?
How did you overcome that feeling?

Have you ever cut someone out of your life? Why? Do you feel you ultimately made the right decision?

Freeze this fucking page. Turn it into an ice cube somehow.
Leave it out in the winter.

When shit doesn't go right, try *fucking left.*

Do you often find yourself **OVERTHINKING** the way you've acted or the things you said in a conversation? Consider the reasons why you might overthink. Are you worried about how others perceive you? Are you guilty of people-pleasing? Are you overly self-critical? (Knock that the fuck off!)

What is your gut reaction to anger?

What are the things you feel?

What are the things you want to do?

Unleash your unbridled fury on this page.

Interpret however the fuck you want.

Too tired for this *bullshit.*

What type of shit embarrasses you? Why?

Nothing on my *give-a-shit* meter.

Having an argument sucks. Losing an argument fucking sucks even more. Use this page to write out any comebacks that occurred to you long after the argument took place.

How do you experience denial? Do you double down and refuse to listen? Do you ignore selective facts that don't support your feelings?

Are there healthier ways to approach this?

ck Up This Journal!

Defy the physics of gravity with this journal.
Toss it in a fucking tree. Jump with it on a trampoline.
Use your damn imagination.

Write about how it feels when you get overwhelmed. How does your body react? What thoughts go through your mind?

Jot down any feelings you're having right now that you'd rather just throw the fuck away. Rip the words off of this page and toss them into the trash, shredder, or even fire if you're feeling fancy.

Don't give a damn.

Are you ever tired of fucking forgiving and forgetting?
What are some thing you will never forgive and/or forget?

Who or what in your life doesn't make you feel heard?

WRITE YOUR ANSWERS IN CAPITAL FUCKING LETTERS.

Give this page (or the whole fucking journal)
a fresh fucking start by throwing it into the laundry.

Yes, this counts as doing chores

Welcome to the *shitshow!*

Sometimes this journal gets lonely.

Loan it to an animal friend for an afternoon.

Let them play fetch with the journal.

What are some things you're just so fucking tired of doing? Or saying? Or hearing?

Hollow out a portion of this journal.

Use the newfound space to store some shit.

Pages for
you to do
whatever the fuck
you want.

If this journal is still intact enough that you can read this fucking page, go back.